FACING YOUR FEARS

H. Norman Wright

POCKET GUIDE ™
Tyndale House Publishers, Inc.
Wheaton, Illinois

Adapted from *Uncovering Your Hidden Fears* by H. Norman Wright, copyright © 1989 by H. Norman Wright.

Scripture quotations, unless otherwise noted, are from *The Holy Bible, New International Version.* Copyright © 1973, 1978, 1984 International Bible Society. Used by permission of Zondervan Bible Publishers.

Scripture quotations marked AMP are from *The Amplified Bible.* Old Testament copyright © 1965, 1987 by The Zondervan Corporation. *The Amplified New Testament* copyright © 1958, 1987 by The Lockman Foundation. Used by permission.

Scripture quotations marked RSV are taken from *The Holy Bible, Revised Standard Version.* Copyright © 1946, 1952, 1971 by the Division of Christian Education of the National Council of the Churches of Christ in the U.S.A. Used by permission.

Pocket Guide is a trademark of Tyndale House Publishers, Inc.

Library of Congress Card Catalog 90-70373
ISBN 0-8423-0825-3
Copyright © 1990 by H. Norman Wright
All rights reserved
Printed in the United States of America

96 95 94 93 92 91
7 6 5 4 3 2

CONTENTS

Are You Keeping Your Fears Alive?

Joan was a middle-aged, well-groomed, successful woman who came to me for counseling. She did not display the normal apprehension that so many people experience during an initial counseling session. She communicated very well, and she was alert and polished in her manner. You would never guess from Joan's appearance and accomplishments the extent of the fear festering inside her which she admitted to me that day.

When I remarked about her outward control and composure, Joan replied, "*No one* is aware of the fear I live with. I am very capable of hiding it."

I asked her, "How is it that a person as capable and successful as you is so wracked by fear? And how have you accomplished so much while carrying such a load of fear?"

Joan's answer amazed me: "That's just it—I'm motivated by fear! Fear drives me; it keeps me going. I don't like being controlled by fear, but I wonder if I would accomplish anything if I were not motivated by it."

Driven by fear. I wonder how many people are driven, like Joan, by the fears of their lives. It seems like such a negative way to be motivated. In some ways a fear-driven life-style can be very effective. But there is a high cost for such a negative drive.

TWO MOTIVATING FORCES

There are two great motivating forces in life: fear and hope. Interestingly, both of these motivators can produce the same results. Fear is a powerful *negative* drive. It compels us forward while inhibiting our progress at the same time. Fear is like a noose that slowly tightens around your neck if you move in the wrong direction. Fear restricts your abilities and thoughts and leads you toward panic reactions. Even when you are standing on the threshold of success, your most creative and inventive plans can be sabotaged by fear.

Fear is also like a videotape continually replaying our most haunting experiences: embarrassing moments, rejections, failures, hurts, disappointments. The message of the fear video is clear: Life is full of these experiences, and they *will* repeat themselves. Fear causes us to say, "I can't do it; I may fail."

Hope is a totally different motivating force—a *positive* drive. Hope is like a magnet that draws you toward your goal. Hope expands your life and brings a message of possibility and change. It draws you away from the bad experiences of the past and toward better experiences in the future. The hope video continually replays scenarios of potential success. Hope causes us to say, "I can do it; I will succeed."

What motivates you? What drives you? What pushes you ahead in life: fear or hope?

THE DESTRUCTIVE POWER OF FEAR
The motivational power of fear is clearly seen in some primitive cultures of the world where voodoo is practiced.

In his book *The Mind/Body Effect,* Dr. Herbert Benson of the Harvard Medical School describes voodoo practices to illustrate the relationship between the human mind and body. Voodoo was originally a form of ancestor worship that is believed to have started in Africa. In the Australian aboriginal tribes, witch doctors often cast voodoo spells on people that led to disease and death. You can imagine the fear that controlled people in these cultures.

Dr. Benson gives a documented example of a young aborigine who slept at a friend's home while on a trip. The young man had been forbidden by his elders to eat wild hen under voodoo threat of death. So at breakfast, the young man asked his older host if the meal he was about to eat was wild hen.

☞ Find Your Fear Type

Imagine that you've received an invitation to a party. You'd like to go to it, but someone who has deeply hurt you in the past will probably also be there. What do you do? Circle your response.

1. Throw away the invitation! Why hassle with the trauma?

2. Decline the invitation. Tell the host or hostess that you had planned to wallpaper your kitchen. Then pull out the wallpaper—*fast!*

3. Mull it over until the day of the party, then decide. Make sure you identify all the worst-case scenarios so you'll be prepared.

4. Call your host or hostess and explain the situation. Maybe he or she can greet you at the door and position you at the opposite side of the room from the acquaintance you want to avoid.

5. Plan to attend the party and don't think twice about it. Try to forget how sick you felt the last time you saw the person you want to avoid.

6. Go to the party but stay only a short time. If you see the other person looking in your direction, make a beeline for the bathroom or the nearest closet.

Now read the section on pages 10-14 that corresponds with your response.

1. Avoider; 2. Silent Martyr;
3. Doomsayer; 4. Manipulator;
5. Noncoper; 6. Runaway

The dish *was* wild hen, but his friend replied, "Of course not." So the young man ate his breakfast and went on his way unaware and unaffected.

Years passed, and once again the two friends met. During their conversation, the older man told his friend about the joke he played on him by serving him wild hen during his visit. The younger man's fears immediately came to the surface. He began to shake with terror, and within twenty-four hours he was dead.[1]

Numerous cases such as this one have been documented over the years. Although it may be an extreme example of the destructive power of fear, it illustrates the negative effect our fears can have on our lives.

HOW DO YOU FEED YOUR FEARS?
In working with fearful clients, I sometimes ask, "What do you do to keep your fear alive?"

Usually their expressions register shock as they respond, "I can't believe you asked me that question! What do you mean 'alive'? I'm trying to kill off my fear, not help it grow! I want it dead and buried."

But I persist with my question. Why? Because most fearful individuals develop behaviors that actually feed their fears. And when a fear is fed, it doesn't diminish—it grows. One of the most important facts to keep in mind about fear is this: *The more you give in to your fears, the more they will grow.*

Fearful people use numerous tactics to keep fear alive. As we consider these characteristic behaviors, see if any of them fits your response to your fears.

The Avoider. Some people work very hard to avoid the object of their fear. One client had a tremendous fear of large trucks. She expended an unbelievable amount of time and energy making sure her route of travel each day was free from trucks. Side streets, out-of-the-way roads, and even alleys became part of her daily itinerary to make sure she avoided meeting any large trucks. Did her avoidance of trucks lessen her fear? No! Her daily ordeal only intensified her fear. Avoiders are motivated by fear.

The Runaway. The runaway will enter the arena of fearful experiences but escape as soon as possible without giving his fear a chance to diminish. A businessman was afraid of business meetings and conventions where others in his profession congregated. He was afraid his peers would discover how inept he was (or thought he was) at his job. But he was required to attend these gatherings. So, tense with fear, he would arrive at a meeting, move quickly through the room to be seen by others, and then quietly leave. Every time he did this his fear increased. And the amount of mental energy he expended on these encounters also intensified his fear. Runaways are motivated by fear.

The Doomsayer. Whenever doomsayers

think about fearful situations, they focus on and exaggerate the worst possible consequences. The possibility of something bad occurring may be extremely remote, but doomsayers always expect problems. Their negativism consumes their attention.

Recently, I heard some examples about partygoers that graphically illustrate the doomsayer's tendencies. Some people are very uncomfortable at parties. When a fearful doomsayer is invited to a party, his fears begin to stir and fester, and he thinks about everything he could do wrong:

- He'll go to the party on the wrong day.
- He'll go to the wrong address.
- He'll arrive too early.
- He'll arrive too late.
- He'll arrive on time, but no other guests will be there, and he will have to carry on a conversation with a boring host.
- He'll be overdressed or underdressed for the occasion.

These are just for starters! Doomsayers also fear their entrance at a party, anticipate spilling food or beverages, dread getting locked in the bathroom, and are nervous about leaving the party gracefully.

When a doomsayer hosts a party, a new range of fears come to light. After the initial fear that no guests will show up, other fears arise:

- The guests will be too early.
- The guests will be too late.

- The early-arriving guests will be wall-flowers, and the conversation will be awkward.
- He will run out of refreshments.
- Some guests will get sick on the hors d'oeuvres.
- He will burn something, and the smoke alarm will sound. Guests will run for the exit; someone will be trampled, break a leg, and sue the host.
- Someone will show up that he didn't invite.
- Someone will show up drunk.

And the list goes on. Ridiculous? Yes, but to some people these fears are very real, stealing the joy from their lives. Doomsayers are motivated by fear.

The Manipulator. This clever individual enlists the help of others as a cushion against fearful situations. One man was terrified of dogs. Before he went to visit friends for the first time, he called in advance to see if they had a dog. If so, he asked the hosts to keep the dog outside or at least out of sight.

Another person was afraid of fainting in elevators. Whenever she had to ride an elevator, she would turn to someone else—whether she knew him or not—and explain her problem. "I tend to pass out in elevators," she explained. "If I appear to be getting dizzy, please take hold of my arm." You can imagine the attention she received every time she stepped into an elevator!

12

Actually, she had never passed out in an elevator, but her fear was real. Manipulators are motivated by fear.

The Noncoper. This person will actually become involved in fearful situations, but his thoughts are consumed by his fear. If he is afraid of crowds, he may be able to enter a room with fifty other people, but he might as well be there alone. He can't tell you about the other people in the room. He is so immobilized in this setting that, if he has some responsibility, he will blow it. He will become tongue-tied, drop whatever he is serving, or forget his thought in the middle of a sentence.

I've been in a number of classrooms where a student stopped cold in the middle of his presentation and stared at his classmates in fright. The inability of these students to cope is usually traced back to the abundance of fear in their minds. That which they feared the most had come upon them—*and they made it happen themselves by plunging unprepared into a fearful situation!* Noncopers are motivated by fear.

The Silent Martyr. The fears of a silent martyr are kept totally hidden from others. Instead of being honest about his fears, this person contrives creative, legitimate-sounding excuses for not participating in a fearful situation. A parent who was deathly afraid of the water could not avoid occasionally taking her children to the beach or to the pool. But she had a vast array of excuses that kept her away from the water:

It was too hot or too cold; she didn't want to risk a sunburn; she preferred to lie around and read; and so forth. Her excuses were certainly reasonable, but they were merely a smoke screen for the sense of terror she had hidden for more than twenty years. And each year, her fear escalated in intensity. Silent martyrs are motivated by fear.[2]

WHAT HAPPENS WHEN YOU SAY "DON'T"

A person who is motivated by fear will think more about what can go wrong than what can go right. This will cause that individual to live defensively, expecting the worst, overreacting, and being immobilized. When you concentrate on what you fear or want to avoid, you increase the likelihood of it happening. Does that sound farfetched? It really isn't.

During the deciding game of the 1950 World Series, Warren Spahn of the Milwaukee Braves was getting ready to pitch to Elston Howard, the power-hitting catcher of the New York Yankees. The Braves' manager walked out to the mound and gave Spahn some simple advice: "Don't pitch him high and outside; he'll knock the ball out of sight." Spahn tried to follow his manager's advice by throwing low and inside. It didn't work. In trying to force his mind away from the feared result, the pitcher could only fulfill the manager's negative advice. Spahn's pitch sailed wide and high in the strike zone, and Elston Howard swatted it over the fence for a home run.

If I asked you *not* to think of the color red for the next two minutes, would you be able to do it? Not really. Your mind would be drawn to red just by the suggestion of it. And the more you feared the consequences of disobeying my request, the more you would struggle to keep your thoughts from gravitating to red. But if I asked you to think of the colors blue and yellow for two minutes, you could do it. And chances are, you wouldn't think of red because the negative suggestion has been replaced by a positive suggestion.

We use negative suggestions all the time. We say to others, "Don't be late," and what happens? We instruct our children, "Don't spill your milk," and what happens? "Don't, don't, don't"—but the words simply reinforce the possibility of the prohibited thought or action actually occurring.

Often when we offer criticism to another person, we do it in a way that subconsciously encourages the negative behavior. And the more we harp on a negative, the greater the likelihood of its occurrence. *But if you point to a desired behavior and spend time and energy talking about it, you increase the chances of that behavior happening.*

MAKE THE LAST THOUGHT COUNT

Actually, the last thought you implant in your mind—or another's mind—usually will grow into the dominant behavior. Since fear peppers our thoughts with negative suggestions, fearful people usually produce fear-ridden behaviors.

For example, everyone feels some fear when encountering a new situation. Some people feel inhibited, crippled, and even paralyzed by fear in the situation, and they behave accordingly. Others move into the situation hopefully, focusing on the positives despite their fears, and they usually succeed. It's basically an attitude problem—our beliefs about ourselves and our outlook on life.

I'm not recommending a self-hype program of unrealistic positive thinking. I am suggesting we steer our attitudes and thoughts *away* from fear-producing negatives and *toward* hope-inspiring positives. One of the best sources of hope-inspiring thoughts is the Bible, and we will refer to it several times in this book.

Believing that you must remain handcuffed and crippled by fear is a myth. You can overcome fear and move ahead in your life!

DO YOU TALK LIKE A VICTIM?

As children we learned certain phrases that seemed innocent. But our belief in these phrases has locked many of us in handcuffs of fear as adults. Here are some examples:

- I can't . . .
- That's a problem.
- I'll never . . .
- That's awful!
- I should . . .
- Why is life this way?
- If only . . .
- Life is a big struggle.
- What will I do?

By using phrases like these, you reinforce the control fear has over your life, and you remain handcuffed in a state of helplessness. You're usually not even aware of what you're doing to yourself. The more you think or say one of these phrases, the more you believe it and the more you fulfill it. You become a victim of your fears. That's why these phrases are called "victim phrases." Let's consider what happens when you use victim phrases.

"I can't..." How many times a day do you say these words? Do you realize these words are prompted by fear?

When you say "I can't," you are saying you have no control over your life. A simple substitution of "I won't" or "I choose not to" at least gives you a choice, perhaps helping you eventually to say "I will" or "I choose to."

"That's a problem." People who see life's complications as problems or burdens are immersed in fear and hopelessness. Life is

full of barriers and detours. But with every obstacle comes an opportunity to learn and grow—if you hold the right attitude. Using other phrases such as "That's a challenge" or "That's an opportunity for learning something new" leaves the door open for moving ahead.

"I'll never . . ." This victim phrase is the anchor of personal stagnation. It's the signal of unconditional surrender to fear. Saying instead, "I've never considered that before" or "I haven't tried it but I'm willing to try" opens the door to personal growth.

"That's awful." Sometimes this phrase is appropriate in view of the shocking, dire situations we often hear about in the day's news. But those events are extraordinary. In everyday experiences, "That's awful" is an inappropriate overreaction that is prompted by fear. Set a goal to eliminate its usage for life's ordinary problems. Instead, respond by saying, "Let's see what we can do about this situation" or "I wonder how we can help at this time."

"I should . . ." This is one of the most controlling statements of all time. Every time you say "I should," you make yourself dependent upon something or someone else. You're at the mercy of whoever taught you the "should." "Should" sounds like an absolute, but it often isn't true or even necessary. Living up to a statement like "I should" is often difficult, and it can drain you emotionally because it generates guilt that then leads to fear. "I could," "It

might be nice to," or "I think I would like to" are healthier statements.

"Why is life this way?" This question is a normal response to the deep pains and sudden shocks of life. But there are those who experience a major tragedy and choose to linger in the stages of shock, withdrawal, and confusion. They inappropriately use this question over and over again.

"Why is life this way?" and its companion statement, "Life isn't fair," are overused for the normal, minor upsets of everyday life. True, life *is* unpredictable and unfair. Life *isn't* always the way we want it to be. But our response to life is our choice, and the healthiest response is reflected in James 1:2-3: "Consider it wholly joyful, my brethren, whenever you are enveloped in or encounter trials of any sort, or fall into various temptations. Be assured and understand that the trial and proving of your faith bring out endurance and steadfastness and patience" (AMP). *Joy in life is a choice.*

"If only . . ." This phrase anchors us to the past and imprisons us in bygone dreams. But the phrase "Next time," shows that we have given up our regrets, we have learned from past occurrences, we have put fear behind us, and we are getting on with our lives.

"Life is a big struggle." This victim phrase reinforces the difficulties of life. Struggles can be and should be turned into adventures. Yes, it will take work. You may be

19

stretched and you may feel uncomfortable. But this is the way to overcome your fear of life's difficulties.

"What will I do?"[3] This question is a cry of despair and fear of the future and the unknown. Instead, say, "I don't know what I can do at this moment, but I know I can handle this. Thank God I don't have to face this issue by myself."

YOU'VE GOTTA HAVE HOPE

My pastor, Lloyd Ogilvie, once said, "If you harbor a fear, you become a landlord for a ghost." Fear will keep you chained to the very problem you are trying to kick out of your life. Fear is not the answer to the problems in your life; hope is the solution. Hope can be cultivated by asking God to set us free from our fears and draw us forward in our lives.

Hope is not blind optimism; it's realistic optimism. A person of hope is always aware of the struggles and difficulties of life, but he lives beyond them with a sense of potential and possibility. A person of hope doesn't just live for the possibilities of tomorrow but sees the possibilities of today, even when his today is not going well. A person of hope doesn't just long for what he's missing in his life but experiences what he has already received. A person of hope can say an emphatic *no* to fear and an energetic *yes* to life.

2

The Fear of Intimacy

The seminar participants filed into the room talking and joking. As they settled into their chairs, a few noticed the statement that had been posted on the front wall. Soon most everybody had seen the statement, and many began to copy it down eagerly. When the seminar leader came in and began the session, he said nothing about the statement. After a while, one man in the group interrupted the leader by saying, "There's a statement on the wall."

The instructor turned, looked at the statement, and said, "Yes, there is," and continued his presentation.

Soon a few other curious hands began to slip up, and another participant asked, "What does that statement mean?"

The instructor stopped and said, "That's an excellent question. How many of you were attracted to this statement?" Most of the group members raised their hands. "You asked me what the statement means, but I have another question. What does it mean to you? You have ten minutes to write your answer to my question." The statement on the wall provoked some furious writing and, later, excellent interaction on the topic of the fear of intimacy.

What was the statement this group couldn't wait to discuss? Perhaps you've heard it before. It's from one of John Powell's books. It reads, "I'm afraid to tell you who I am because you might not like who I am and that's all I've got."

THE MEANING OF INTIMACY

The fear of not being liked is a strong inhibitor of intimacy and closeness. On the one hand, we have a need for intimacy, but on the other hand, we often suffer from an immobilizing fear that resists closeness. We want to be close, but we are afraid of being rejected, losing the love or respect of others, or discovering something we didn't wish to know about ourselves. We are afraid of being embarrassed.

To understand this fear, we have to understand intimacy, the source of our fear. Intimacy is the foundation for both love and friendship. It's a close emotional bond that involves mutual sharing and understanding.

Please note the word *mutual*. Each partner in an intimate relationship wants to know the other person's deepest dreams, wishes, concerns, hopes, and fears while at the same time being an open book himself. Intimacy leads to deep feelings of closeness, warmth, and trust. Intimacy eliminates the pain of loneliness and the pain of being strangers with one another. And there is no greater pain than being strangers in your own marriage. If you're going to have intimacy in your relationship, you must have the confidence to expose the private, vulnerable portion of your life. Intimacy means you cannot remain isolated from another.[1]

But sometimes intimacy hurts. Vulnerability carries with it the risk of being painfully real with another person. Mike Mason says:

> It is not intimacy itself, therefore, which is so distasteful and intimidating to the world, but rather the moral condemnation that comes with it. People crave closeness with one another but are repelled by the sin that such closeness inevitably uncovers in themselves, the selfish motives that are unmasked, the pettiness that spills out, the monstrous new image of self that emerges as it struggles so pitifully to have its own way.[2]

There are many who choose to be lonely to avoid the pain of developing intimacy. They are afraid of other people. It is an overwhelming task for them to reach out to others. Those who have experienced intimacy find it difficult to fathom this fear of closeness. Why would someone feel apprehensive about being emotionally close to another person?

23

One main reason is low self-esteem. If you constantly criticize yourself, you probably will fear that other people will follow your example and criticize you too. As one female client confessed, "When a man starts getting close, I run. I just know he's going to become critical of me. I'm enough of a critic of myself. I don't need his criticism." And the fear of seeing her own criticism come through another person keeps her blocked. If you want to be vulnerable to another person and experience love and closeness, you have to accept and love yourself.

WHY WOMEN FEAR INTIMACY

Women fear intimate relationships for several reasons. One primary fear is the pain of rejection. Kimberly was a young divorcée who was attempting to make the adjustment back into single life. She complained:

> I poured myself into that relationship for six years. I held nothing back, thinking my openness would make the marriage. It didn't. I feel abandoned and emotionally raped. I gave and he took. Then I got left behind. Why care that much?

Yes, it does hurt when intimate relationships fall apart. But when there is *no* intimacy and closeness in a relationship, there is an *even greater chance* of a relationship dissolving! When you insulate yourself against others, you tend to bring about that which you fear the most—abandonment. The courage to run the risk of intimacy can bring tremendous fulfillment in life for both men and women.

Women also struggle with the fear of losing their identity in an intimate relationship with a man. Even though women tend to encourage and be more comfortable with intimacy than men, some women fear losing their sense of independence and autonomy if they get too close to their man.

We all need our own space, our privacy, and our separateness. That's normal. But some women are afraid a man's demands for closeness and sharing may become too energy-draining for them. They fear their men may begin to invade their lives too much. And in some cases, if a man is vulnerable and discloses his deepest feelings, both positive and negative, she fears he might be weak and unable to give her the care she desires.

WHY MEN FEAR INTIMACY
It is rare to find a man who doesn't have some struggles with intimacy. Men love the benefits of intimacy, but often they are not committed to the work intimacy entails. Though few of them will admit it, most men fear intimacy, and this fear is reflected in the way they interact with their wives, families, and friends.

☞ What Some Men Say about Intimacy

Why is it men avoid intimacy? Listen to a few of their responses, all of which reflect rationalizations rather than actual reasons:

"That's just the way men are. We aren't intimate the way women are."

"We don't know any differently. It's good enough for us. We're satisfied with it. You can't really show us a better way."

"If you open up and share your feelings, others will take advantage of you. It's just not safe."

"You can't be macho and vulnerable at the same time. It doesn't work, and I wouldn't know how to learn anyway."

"The main reason I can't be intimate is that when I try, my wife is the judge of whether or not I've shared a true feeling. I really *do* try to open up and get close as she asks. But there's got to be a list of rules about feelings and closeness somewhere that only women know. From her perspective, I never get it right."

"I don't think women want men to be vulnerable. When we show feelings more, they don't know what to do. They can't handle it."

"I don't know whether or not I'm comfortable telling her everything. If I did something to make her mad, she'd use it against me. She has shared some things with her friends that I thought were only between the two of us. That hurt."

A major concern for men about intimacy with women is trust. Some men have had bad experiences after opening themselves up to the women in their lives. *Who* can be trusted? *When* can they be trusted? *What* can they be trusted with? Many men believe women perceive information differently and they share in public what men see as personal.

Another concern of men has its roots in the issue of control. When a man shares his personal thoughts and feelings in order to draw close to someone, he is potentially giving that person influence over him. That individual can use the information shared either *for* his welfare or *against* his welfare. It's risky. So withholding information helps a man retain a sense of control over his life and gain power over others.[3]

Many men fear losing this power over themselves and others. Research confirms that men withhold information about themselves in order to mislead others and often misrepresent themselves to others. Listen to what women have said about men and openness:

"I really don't know how he feels."

"He knows why he does what he does. But he doesn't tell me anything; he just does it."

"Sometimes I think that's just the way men are."

"I'm really puzzled about how to respond to him."

"Apparently, men need to think about how they feel."

"I'm not sure men know how they are supposed to feel."

But look at what men have said about themselves and openness:

"I don't really know how I feel at times."

"Who knows why I do what I do? It just happens."

"That's just the way I am."

"Honestly, I don't always know how to react."

"I have to think about how I feel before I express it."

"I don't know what I am supposed to feel."

Men often keep their thoughts and feelings a mystery in order to control the responses of others to them. But treating themselves as mysteries also helps men handle another fear they rarely admit to: the fear of really knowing themselves. When a man withholds information about himself from other people, he can avoid facing his own inconsistencies and inadequacies.

So avoiding intimacy is a controlling behavior that "helps" a man in two ways. First, it gives him the power over others that he associates with success in life. Second, it serves as protection against exposing his frailties to himself. Once again, we see how fear can drive a person.

THE CONSEQUENCES
OF INDEPENDENCE

A growing body of research shows that men who live in isolation through a lack of intimacy suffer a definite decline in both physical and mental health. The absence of close, caring relationships is a source of stress for men. Elderly men have the highest suicide rate of all age groups, and stress is often the culprit. Heart attacks and cancer, the number one and number two killers of men, also have been tied into stress.

Cultivating social support is one of the best ways to handle the stress of life. Intimacy can modify or actually eliminate stressful circumstances in a man's life. Perhaps one way to override the fear of intimacy is to consider the health benefits—specifically, stress reduction—intimacy can provide.

Fortunately, today many men are breaking out of their fears and discovering that sharing their problems with others creates an atmosphere for problem solving. As men share their personal thoughts, feelings, and concerns with others, they realize the caring atmosphere helps them explore alternatives and solutions to their problems more clearly. Intimacy is actually a means to a greater level of efficiency.[4]

Furthermore, when a man relates closely to others, he discovers a greater awareness of himself. Fears can be dissolved, and a healthy level of self-acceptance has an opportunity to develop.

Some men approach intimacy with reservations, saying, "If I do start to confront my fear of intimacy and open up, I need several things to keep myself going. I need to see there are more benefits in opening up than in staying closed. I need to see it's safe to open up. I don't want any negative value judgments about what I'm sharing. Nor do I want others telling me their opinion of what I think or feel inside. I need others to tell me it's OK to do this."

Men, be encouraged that others like you are hesitant about developing intimacy in relationships. It is a slow journey. It takes work and time. It involves a level of discomfort. It involves taking in more information about feelings. And it may involve participating in a small group of men who are willing to embark upon this same journey. But as one man who made the journey stated, "What was there to be afraid of in the first place? There are other things in life more terrifying than intimacy, and I've faced them. I guess I created my fear in the first place."

☞Books for Men

Three books can make a difference for a man who wants to develop intimacy:

- *The Secrets Men Keep* by Dr. Ken Druck (Ballantine Books)
- *Men Have Feelings Too* by G. Brian Jones (Victor Books)
- *The McGill Report on Male Intimacy* by Michael McGill (Harper and Row).

WHY COUPLES FEAR COMMITMENT

The fear of intimacy has impacted marriage statistics in our nation in the form of the fear of commitment. Many men and women are hesitant to take the step of commitment necessary for marriage.

It's true, there is a need for being cautious in our commitments. But the fear of commitment causes some to hesitate and hesitate and hesitate, and the longer they wait, the greater the fear becomes.

When it comes down to making a relationship permanent through commitment, the subtle "what if" germ begins to invade our minds. "What if I'm attracted to someone else after I'm married?" "What if this isn't God's will for my life?" "What if I commit myself and the relationship fails?" "What if I commit myself and I get hurt?" Endless "what if" questions keep many couples from the commitment and intimacy that help make a marriage strong.

Tim Timmons and Charlie Hedges talk about three of the major fears of commitment. First, there is the fear of giving love without receiving love in return. We all want to receive love in the same measure we give it. And in a marriage, giving without receiving is very painful.

Second, the fear of being used and taken advantage of is an inhibitor to commitment, especially after one partner gives personal information about himself.

Third, one of the most paralyzing fears preventing commitment is desertion.

Desertion is the ultimate form of rejection. Anyone who has been jilted in the past always has the fear of desertion lurking in the back of his mind, blocking future commitments.[5]

RISK YOUR WAY OUT OF FEAR

What can you do about your fear of intimacy? Take a risk! Learn a new way to respond to the fear that causes you to shrink away from enriching, intimate relationships. Face your fear and override it.

The word *risk* may strike fear in your heart, but risking is the only way to grow. Taking a risk for intimacy means you will have to give up some false beliefs. For example, you must give up believing that intimacy always leads to hurt or that someone will take advantage of you.

You may feel somewhat empty for the false beliefs you leave behind. You can fill the void with the confidence that comes from a personal relationship with God through Jesus Christ. Fill it with the truths of the Bible. Fill it with the many encouragements that are found in Scripture. Read Isaiah 41:10 and 43:15, for example.

And when you begin to build an intimate relationship, move slowly and ask questions that come to mind. But at some point, take the risk to make a commitment in the relationship.

I like the illustration David Viscott gives concerning the risk of making a commitment. He calls it the point of no return and compares it to passing a car on a two-lane highway. When preparing to pass, you first assess the possibilities of passing, then you select the time and place, gather the momentum and power, and move out. When you hit the accelerator, you have taken a carefully calculated risk and have passed the point of no return. If you sense you're in danger after pulling out, hesitating and backing off will usually lead to an accident. But accelerating, sounding your horn, and creating a safe place for yourself is the best course.

Similarly, in intimacy you must carefully assess the relationship and make a commitment. True, once you commit yourself and pass the point of no return, there is a greater possibility of being hurt. But you also have a greater possibility of succeeding in a relationship than you did before you risked the commitment.[6]

☞ Checkpoint

To help you conquer your fears and develop intimacy, complete the following exercise on a separate sheet of paper for one or more of your close relationships:

1. The type of relationship I would like with this person is . . .
2. The advantages of developing intimacy with this individual are . . .
3. What might happen if I commit myself to this person?
4. Does this person feel the same about our relationship as I do?
5. What are his/her thoughts about intimacy?
6. What do I want from this person?
7. Does he/she have the ability to give me what I want?
8. Who are the other people I have been close to in the past?
9. How did I benefit from being close to them?
10. What is the fear I may be experiencing now?
11. How much do I care about this person's feelings?
12. What are my feelings?
13. Does he/she care about my feelings?
14. What is my level of trust in this person?
15. What have I shared with this person about my feelings?
16. Two examples of sharing deep feelings with this person in the past are . . .

17. The results of sharing these feelings were . . .
18. What would happen if this person were not a part of my life?
19. Does this person need me?
20. What would I be most willing to share about myself with this person?
21. What would I be most hesitant to share with this person?
22. What is there about me that would disappoint or hurt this person if he knew?
23. What are five expectations I have for this person?
24. What are five expectations he/she has for me?
25. Topics we tend to avoid are . . .
26. Do I act real in this relationship? Why or why not?
27. How much is my self-esteem built upon this relationship?
28. We pray together when . . .
29. The indications that God is for this relationship are . . .
30. The way I pray for this person is . . .
31. The way I have been praying for this relationship is . . .
32. What it will take for me to risk greater openness and intimacy in this relationship now is . . .
33. What I intend to do now with this relationship is . . .[7]

The Fear of Losing Control

Our raft was floating in the center of a swiftly flowing river that was about thirty feet wide. We steered the raft carefully around the boulders that jutted out of the water every few yards.

Then it happened. As we swept around a curve in the river, we saw another stream dead ahead that was pouring a torrent of water into our channel. We had been in control of our raft up to that point. But where the tributary merged with the main channel, the turbulence was more than we could handle. No effort at steering or slowing down worked. For several minutes we were at the mercy of the two raging rivers, enduring the frightful experience of being completely out of control.

The fearful, out-of-control feeling can envelop you anytime and anyplace. It can occur suddenly and unexpectedly—or so gradually you don't realize what's happening. One minute you're walking carefully on ice and snow, the next you're flying through the air toward a painful encounter with the ground. Or you're sitting in a

37

meeting you have called for your own purposes but begin to realize it isn't going the way you had hoped. Or you're driving on the freeway and need to move into the right lane to make your exit. You signal and look for an opening in the traffic, but the other drivers are unwilling to let you change lanes. You helplessly watch your exit pass by.

OUR NEED TO FEEL IN CONTROL

Even though we express it in various ways, we all feel the need to be in control. For some, being in control is the driving, dominant force in their lives. For all of us, the amount of stress we experience is directly related to how much we feel we are in control of our lives and circumstances.

At the heart of this concern over control is fear. One of the greatest contributors to stress in men is the fear of feeling out of control. Though a woman may admit to this fear, a man rarely will because such a humbling confession adds to his tension.

Yet one of the most common fears in life is that of losing control. The things we value most are the very things we feel we must have control over: power, prestige, a person, a job, status, and so forth. One who fears the loss of control becomes almost desperate in his attempts to stay in control.

Here are some facts about control and fear:

- If you are in a pressure-filled or undesirable situation *by choice,* you often will feel challenged or stimulated by it. But if that negative circumstance was thrust upon you or was not of your own choosing, it will be more stressful than challenging. Underlying the stress is the fear of being out of control.
- A man who quits his job feels like he retains control of his career; a man who is fired fears he has lost that control. A woman who chooses a job transfer to a new city feels she still has control of her situation; when she is told to transfer or lose her job, she feels out of control.
- When you can anticipate the consequences of a situation and foresee a bit of the future, you feel more in control. When the outcome of events in your life is unpredictable, the underlying stressful fear of being out of control can be present.

PORTRAIT OF A CONTROLLER

The controlling person makes it a point to be in control at all times. Slavish rigidity to rules—for himself and those around him—is the controller's life-style. The controller is only comfortable when he knows the outcome to everything, when the limits of life are clearly defined, and when there are no surprises.

Some extreme controllers constantly check and double-check to make sure nothing will go wrong. And when something *does* go haywire, the controller increases rigidity and attention to detail in order to bring life back under control. For most of these people, relationships take second place to order and routine. Details, structure, and lists become their bywords and their security.

Have you met anyone who comes across as domineering and controlling? If so, you've encountered someone motivated by fear. I've shared that truth with married couples sitting in my counseling office, especially when one partner is the overbearing, dominant type. When I initially raise the possibility of the controlling spouse being motivated by fear, I often hear disbelief in the response of the dominated partner. "Fear?" one wife retorted. "There's not a shred of fear in that man. He doesn't give others a chance. From the minute he meets them, he let's them know he's in charge. And anyone who shows any sign of controlling him is dominated immediately."

I responded to her by suggesting, "Perhaps his controlling nature is his way of never allowing anyone to get close enough to discover that he's afraid." She left my office with a new perspective on her domineering husband.

Controlling people strive for the appearance of being in control, but inwardly they live in fear. Many of them feel they cannot control their own feelings, so they attempt to control the way other people feel. They desperately want others to love them. But it's risky for controllers to give others the choice to love them (because they may choose *not* to!), so they instead demand love from others.

☞Are You Controlled by Fear?

Circle the statements below that describe you.

1. I hate it when things go wrong.
2. I think many mistakes could be avoided by checking and doublechecking the facts.
3. I prefer to know what's expected of me.
4. I like to take charge of a situation.
5. I make and use lists frequently.
6. I plan my weekends well before Friday.
7. I feel angry when someone disagrees with me.
8. It's hard for me to admit that I'm wrong.
9. I often feel alone and isolated even though I have friends.
10. I feel uncomfortable unless I know or can make the rules of a situation.
11. I have a hard time being spontaneous.
12. I don't like to lose.

If you circled more than six of the above statements, you may be controlled by fear.

CONTROL IN DISGUISE

For some controllers, every day is Halloween because they must constantly hide their fears behind acceptable social disguises. These disguises are often ineffective and even harmful, but controllers feel they must mask their fears from others. Let's look at a few of these disguises.

The disguise of strength. In order to appear competent to others, fearful controllers try to appear strong. Physical strength and strength of character are admirable qualities, but they need to be genuine. Strength as a disguise often comes across as being overbearing and controlling, not genuine.

Once you portray this picture of strength, you lock yourself into a performance and can never be yourself. You actually allow others to control and dominate you by forcing you to look strong. In order to appear strong, you can never let down or back off. You always have to be up. It's also difficult to sit back, relax, and enjoy whatever success you have found. Your fears drive you always to stay ahead of others and set the pace.

This disguise of strength denies you the opportunity to enjoy others. How can you, since you are constantly comparing yourself to others in order to appear the strongest? What's worse, your show of strength doesn't help your fear disappear.

The disguise of love. Have you ever been smothered by an overly loving person? These individuals want the best for their loved ones. At first glance, they appear generous, and they openly share their concern for others.

But their love is really a mask hiding their fear of losing someone close to them. The fear of abandonment drives people to control their loved ones, but these efforts usually fail. And when controllers become aware of the lack of affection from their loved ones, few have the wisdom to back off and allow their loved ones to love them by choice. Unfortunately, controllers tend to be possessive, which further drives others away.

The disguise of procrastination. Have you ever been involved with a procrastinator— perhaps a friend, a family member, or even yourself? We tend to think of a procrastinator as someone who doesn't have all his ducks lined up in a row or whose mind is floating around the universe somewhere. But procrastinators are real, sane people whose behavior creates problems for themselves and others.

Procrastination is often only a symptom. Telling a procrastinator to "get with it" or to "get organized" is a monologue in futility. You need to understand why the procrastinator procrastinates. There are several reasons, and one of them is the desire to feel in control.

Many procrastinators feel an intense sense of independence. They procrastinate in order to demonstrate that no one can force them to do what they don't want to do. The procrastinator's behavior says,

"You can't make me do it. I'm in control." It's the cry of the strong-willed adult! The procrastinator will do what he wants to do when he is good and ready, not when someone else tells him to do it.

The disguise of a martyr. Some people use the martyr approach to control others. They attempt to impose an excessive amount of responsibility on others through comments like:

- "Look at everything I've done for you."
- "You don't really care about anyone but yourself."
- "So this is how you thank me. I feel rejected."
- "You're not coming to visit me on vacation? I hope you enjoy yourself, even though I won't have a very good time."
- "It's your decision, but if you'd listen to me, you wouldn't have so many problems."
- "I make the money. Why shouldn't I decide how we spend it?"
- "When you have children, I hope they treat you better than you've treated me."
- "You ought to be ashamed of the way you've been neglecting me."

CONTROL IN MARRIAGE

Some people want to make all the decisions in their marriages, and they demand to be in control of their spouses. When disagreements occur, power struggles develop. And the controlling partner uses numerous tactics to maintain control, including put-downs, intimidation, threats, a loud voice, and silence. The controller doesn't stop to consider the negative effect of his or her behavior. In time, the affection of the controller's partner begins to diminish, even though he or she may be well provided for in other areas. As one person put it, "Who falls in love with his jailor?"

A controlling person is unable to relate to his partner intimately. Controllers insist on being right, on winning, and on showing that others are wrong. They have great difficulty accepting blame. They profess expertise in too many areas and, because of their need to appear perfect, they cannot take criticism gracefully. Because of this behavior, they often feel unappreciated, especially by their spouses. Others give up in their attempts to love them since there is no real vulnerability.

Controlling people often feel alone and isolated even in their own marriages. But they are responsible for their condition. They have blocked off the positive emotional areas of their lives, and they have trod heavily on the feelings of others. They end up feeling hurt, wounded, rejected, and neglected. Do they admit their hurt? Not usually. Pain is not easy to admit, so this feeling often turns into anger, which feeds the tendency to control.[1]

CONTROL AND SPIRITUALITY
Some people take control in their lives because they fear the control, influence, or

direction of others. They're afraid of not being in charge of their own destiny. They would tend to boast, "I know what's best for me. I have all the knowledge and skill necessary to direct my life."

I wonder how controllers like these get along with God. I wonder how they try to determine God's will for their lives (or maybe that question never enters their minds). I wonder how controllers handle the unexpected and uncontrollable crises of life and learn to view these upsets with a spiritual perspective. I wonder how they learn to trust Jesus Christ as Savior. A controller has difficulty trusting God because he fears the control of his life resting in anyone's hands but his own.

On the issue of control and fear as it relates to spiritual life, Lloyd Ogilvie states:

> Our need to be in charge of ourselves, others, and situations often makes our relationship with Christ life's biggest power struggle. We are reluctant to relinquish our control and allow Him to run our lives. We may believe in Him and be active in the church and Christian causes, but trusting Him as Lord of everything in life can be scary. Even though we pray about our challenges and problems, all too often what we really want is strength to accomplish what we've already decided is best for ourselves and others.
>
> Meanwhile, we press on with our own priorities and plans. We remain the scriptwriter, casting director, choreographer, and

☞ Thirty Days to Trust

Week 1. On a separate sheet of paper, describe the areas of your life in which you feel you must be in control. List statements you use to maintain control. Then brainstorm and identify the underlying fears that cause you to seek control.

Take several minutes each day to pray about your fears. Set up two chairs facing each other. Sit in one of the chairs and pray aloud, talking to the empty chair as though God were sitting there. Describe for Him what you've written, and tell Him about your fears. Ask Him what you should do about them.

Week 2. Begin each day with prayer admitting that you have a need to depend upon God rather than yourself for control in your life. Extend your hands upward, symbolically giving your fears to God. Imagine Him receiving your fears and offering to help you.

Week 3. Identify one area where you will give up some control each day. For example, you may decide to ask others for their opinions on issues and do what they suggest instead of asserting your opinion.

At the end of each day, write down your experiences for the day. Describe how you relinquished control, how you felt before and after, and what the benefits were or will be.

Week 4. Repeat the procedure for week 3, focusing on another area where you want to give up control each day.

producer of the drama of our own lives, in which we are the star performer.[2]

Do you relate to what he said? Do you identify with any part of it? Many do.

It's true that trusting another person—even God—is risky. Living by faith may be a new experience for you. But living a life of faith in Jesus Christ is far less risky than living a life of faith in yourself. Trying to control your life imprisons you in the need to be in control. Trusting in His ability to control leads to a life of freedom rather than a life of bondage.

You never were in total control! You never will be in total control! Why stay in bondage to the myth that you must be in control? There's a better way to live.

I'm not asking you to give up your lifestyle of control. All I'm asking you to do is to place the control of your life in Christ's hands for thirty days (see page 47). Weigh the results, then decide which way you would prefer to live. It's really your choice.

Surrender your will to God's will and commit your total life—all that you are and have—to Him. God wants the best for you. It's clearly stated in His Word, the Bible. Read it and you will discover He promises you His wisdom for your decisions, His supernatural strength for your challenges, and His love for your relationships. That's not a bad offer!

The Fear of Failure

Years ago, there was a TV game show in which contestants could choose unseen prizes from behind one of five doors on stage. Behind some of the doors were silly or embarrassing prizes like a bucket of Jell-O or a pool of slimy mud. But behind one of the doors was a brand new Chevrolet Camaro.

It was interesting to watch how different types of contestants made their choices. Bold contestants looked at all the doors, confidently made a selection, opened a chosen door, and accepted the consequences graciously—good prize or bad. They didn't hesitate, and they weren't intimidated by the possibility of making the wrong decision.

Wishy-washy contestants looked at one door and then another, started toward one, stopped, went toward another, hesitated, and then, just before time ran out, plunged through the nearest door. But often, when the wishy-washy contestants found a worthless prize on the other side of a door, they were very upset. Sometimes you could hear them berating themselves for their bad decision.

Then there were the paralyzed contestants. They were unable to make a choice. They were so immobilized by the fear of making a wrong decision that the allotted time expired and they lost the opportunity to choose. "I just can't make up my mind," they would say. "I can't choose." Wrong! They did choose! How? By *not* choosing, they chose to lose.

People often choose to lose by failing to make decisions. When we were children, our parents cautioned us with the words "Be careful not to make the wrong decision." And some of us still live by that creed. We are paranoid about making the right decisions. Wrong decisions, we reason, bring ridicule, embarrassment, and numerous negative consequences. So instead of risking a wrong decision, we make no decision, and, like the paralyzed contestants on the game show, we get nothing.

The fear of making a wrong decision reflects a lack of trust and self-confidence. It is just one example of a common intimidating restraint—the fear of failure.

NOBODY WANTS TO FAIL

Failure—the very word ignites an uncomfortable feeling within most of us. We don't want to think about failure, much less experience it. The fear of failing drives some people to rounds of relentless activity where satisfaction is never achieved. The fear of failing inhibits many others from stepping out and making progress. They live their lives mired in dissatisfaction, but they are unwilling to leave the safe confines of their stagnation because they are afraid they will only sink deeper into failure.

I've been afraid of failing, haven't you? Do you remember the teacher coming up to you and saying, "I'm sorry, you failed the exam." Can you recall the sinking feeling in the pit of your stomach when you saw the large, dark *F* on your report card? I can. Your entire world turned dark, especially when someone faced you with a smile and asked, "How did *your* grades turn out?"

What about the political candidate who invests enormous sums of money and hundreds of hours in a campaign—and loses? Failure! What about the creative time and thought that goes into the proposal you present to one of your clients—and they choose a competitor? Failure! What about the vast amounts of time, money, and emotion invested in courting someone you love—only to hear a firm no to your proposal of marriage? Failure!

Nobody enjoys failing. We all want to succeed and achieve. When we fail, we see ourselves as unsuccessful, perhaps even deficient or not good enough. There must be something wrong with us, we conclude; that's why we failed!

FAILURE AND THE SEXES

The fear of failure is a major stress point for men. Men have a great need to achieve and, as we have seen, to feel they are in control. The fact that everyone makes mistakes is of little comfort to men in their moments of failure. Their competitive tendencies drive them to succeed for fear they will be dominated by others. Often their identities are so closely tied to their jobs that failing at work is tantamount to failing as a person.

For a man, admitting fear can be traumatic since it implies he is vulnerable and out of control. Emotional control is a high value in many cultures' concepts of masculinity. Since men don't like to acknowledge their fears, whenever they do seek counseling, their problems are often more intense than a woman's.

Many men translate their fear response into anger. Admitting fear draws people close, and intimacy may be too threatening. But anger helps create a distance between a man and the people he fears. Anger can be a mask he hopes will intimidate others and fool them into thinking he is in control. Anger is the camouflage many men use to hide their fears.*

The fear of failure pressures men to create a reservoir of excuses to avoid failure and remain in control. Have you heard (or used) any of the following excuses ?

* For additional information on this subject, see chapter 8 in my book *Understanding the Man in Your Life* (Word Books).

- John avoided failure by putting things off. He would delay and stall on his tasks so he could say, "I had too little time, and that kept me from doing a better job."
- Sam tended to constantly overschedule himself. He would say, "I just have too much to do. No one could possibly keep up with everything that's been dumped on me."
- Jim made everything he did extremely difficult. He always looked for the hardest way to complete a task. It was a great excuse to hide his fear of failure. After all, who could succeed with so many difficult tasks?
- Frank was a competent thirty-year-old man with a good work record, but his superiors were mystified over his refusal to complete the forms and procedures for a promotion. Frank was afraid of getting turned down for a new position, so he always found an excuse not to apply. He would rather stay in the safety of his present position.

I've heard many men (and women too) finally admit that it is less painful not to try than to try and fail!

Women also have a fear of failure, but much of it has been linked with the female's cultural legacy of nonassertiveness and passivity. Georgia Watkin-Lanoil, author of *The Female Stress Syndrome,* feels a woman's fear of failure is the result of years of being shamed or teased by men whenever she attempted a public performance of athletic, mechanical, or combative skill. It is fairly common, however, for a woman to feel both the need to achieve and the fear of failure at the same time. But fear tends to prevail and immobilize a woman because of her excessive concern over the opinions of others. And as this concern is often at its peak when she's with men, a woman collects an array of excuses for her failure to use when needed.[1]

UNDERSTANDING
THE PERFECTIONIST

The fear of failure is alive and well in those whom you would never suspect. A perfectionist is such a person. The perfectionist has a self-critic dwelling within him. He strives to do the impossible, places unrealistic demands on himself, and, when he is unable to meet those demands, feels overwhelmed. The perfectionist expects more of himself than he can attain.

Perfectionism is driven by a familiar underlying force—the fear of failure. This fear causes perfectionists to live in a highly cautious, guarded manner. When a perfectionist is disappointed by his performance on a task, he doesn't think he has failed just on that task. He thinks he has failed as a person.

Many perfectionists operate on the following formula:

1. What I produce is a reflection of how much ability I have.

2. My level of ability determines my worth as a person.

3. What I'm able to attain reflects my worth as a person.

4. Failure means I'm not worth much.

And so the fear of failure becomes a motivating force in the perfectionist's life.

To avoid failure, most perfectionists protect themselves by living in such a way that makes them appear anything but perfect: They procrastinate. As one man said, "If my best shot isn't going to make it, I'm not even going to try until I'm assured of success. I can't face being a failure, and I don't want the whole world to know."

PROCRASTINATION: TOOL OF FEAR

Procrastination comes from two Latin words, *pro,* meaning "forward" and *cras,* meaning "the morrow." Literally, to procrastinate means to put something forward till the morrow—or, as we often quip, "Don't do today what you can put off till tomorrow." One author described procrastination as "the burglar of time, a thief which robs today of freedom and fills tomorrow with frustration."[2] But the perfectionist doesn't see procrastination this way because his procrastination is serving a purpose. The perfectionist's motto is, "Do it later when you have a better chance to succeed."

Procrastination is a comfort to some people because it allows them to believe their ability is greater than their performance might be. After all, by procrastinating, you never really have to find out! Who wants to discover he *can't* do it when it's so much less painful to put it off and think he *can* do it? Meanwhile, he has a built-in excuse for his failure: "If I went ahead and tackled this project, it would be a breeze. But I just have so many other things taking up my time."

The driving fear of failure is so strong that many perfectionists are willing to accept the consequences of procrastination. Admitting to laziness or disorganization is less painful than admitting to inadequacy.

A perfectionist is the type of person who will paint himself into a corner. He limits himself by erroneously believing there is only one correct solution to a problem and he must find it. This is where procrastination enters in. Perfectionists are reluctant to act or commit to anything until they've discovered the correct solution. Some perfectionists make extensive lists of pros and cons, evaluate them, and then make more lists. But no matter how many factors are considered, final action—and the dreaded failure—are perpetually delayed.

THE HOPE OF ADEQUACY

We may as well accept it: You and I will never be perfect. If we are perfectionists, we will always be imperfect perfectionists. Why? Because the perfect world God created was marred by the Fall, and we can never regain through our own efforts what was lost.

Even knowing that, perfectionistic Christians continue to live as though they could perform perfectly. But it's impossible. Because of the Fall, we lost natural and ecological perfection, physical perfection, mental perfection, emotional perfection, relational perfection, and spiritual perfection. We've lost a lot! And no matter how much we strive through our own efforts, we can't earn what has already been lost.3

Remember that a perfectionistic person is a driven person, one who, upon making an outstanding accomplishment, cannot enjoy the results. He is like a pole-vaulter in a major track meet. Every time the bar is raised, he clears it successfully. Gradually, his competitors are eliminated, and he wins the event. But does he rest and savor his victory? No. He asks the officials to raise the bar three inches higher. He tries and tries and tries to clear the bar, but fails each time. He feels terrible; he has failed. He cannot experience the joy of winning first place. He must do better. Unfortunately, many people are like this dissatisfied pole-vaulter.

If you are a Christian perfectionist, part of your struggle is the cry of desperation that rises within you: "What if I fail? What if I'm not perfect?" Relax! I have an answer for you:

- You have failed in the past.
- You are failing now in some way.
- You will fail in the future.
- You weren't perfect in the past.
- You aren't perfect now.
- You won't be perfect in the future.

I like what David Seamands says about the issue of Christians and failure:

> To ask the question, "What if I fail?" is once again to attach strings to God's unconditional love and to change the nature of grace as undeserved and unearned favor. If your failure could stop grace, there would never be any such thing as grace. For the ground of grace is the cross of Christ, and on the cross we were all judged as total failures. It was not a question of an occasional failure here and there. As far as our ability to bridge the moral canyon and win the approval of a Holy God, we are all total failures. In the Cross we were all examined and we all flunked completely![4]

You see, in spite of being a failure and not being perfect, you and I are loved and accepted by God. Seamands adds:

> God's love for us is unconditional; it is not a love drawn from God by something good in us. It flows out of God because of His nature. God's love is an action toward us, not a reaction to us. His love depends not on what we are but on what He is. He loves because He is love. We can refuse the love of God, but we

cannot stop Him from loving us. We can reject it and thus stop its inflow into us, but we can do nothing to stop its outflow from Him. Grace is the unconditional love of God in Christ freely given to the sinful, the undeserving, and the imperfect.[5]

Failure will always be with us in this life. It's all right; it's normal. It's part of being human. When you fail, allow yourself to feel disappointment but not disapproval. When you release your grip on perfectionism, the fear of failure will release its grip on you. *

DON'T QUIT BEFORE TRYING
We all encounter tasks or problems in life that appear impossible. And when we face these mountains of impossibility, we are tempted to give up even before we try to scale them because we're convinced we will fail. But we quit before considering God's perspective of our situation. We're afraid we can't do anything and that God can't do anything, and so we do nothing.

I have found a scriptural example that I think applies to our fear of failure. The following event took place shortly after Moses led the nation of Israel out of Egypt:

The Egyptians—all Pharaoh's horses and chariots, horsemen and troops—pursued the Israelites and overtook them as they camped by the sea near Pi Hahiroth, opposite Baal Zephon. As Pharaoh approached, the Israelites

---

* For additional information on this subject, see chapter 8 in my book *Understanding the Man in Your Life* (Word Books).

looked up, and there were the Egyptians, marching after them. They were terrified and cried out to the Lord. (Exodus 14:9-10)

The Israelites faced a seemingly impossible situation, and they were afraid. Their fear prompted them to complain to Moses, angrily blaming him for the apparent failure to which they had already conceded. They even said they would rather serve the Egyptians than die in the wilderness.

But listen to what Moses said to the people:

Do not be afraid. Stand firm and you will see the deliverance the Lord will bring you today. The Egyptians you see today you will never see again. The Lord will fight for you; you need only to be still. (Exodus 14:13-14)

Notice the steps of direction given in this passage:

1. "Do not be afraid." Lloyd Ogilvie suggests:

Fear is usually the first reaction to our impossibility. Don't be afraid of fear. It reminds us we are alive, human. Like pain, it's a megaphone shout for God—a prelude to faith. The same channel of our emotions through which fear flows can be the riverbed for trust and loving obedience. Fear is only a hairbreadth away from faith. When we surrender our fear, telling God how we feel, we allow faith to force out fear. Tell God, "I'm afraid. I don't understand what you are doing with me! But I know there is something greater than this fear I feel. I know that you are in control and will allow nothing which will not bring me into deeper communion with you. What you give or take away is done that I might know you better." That's courageous praying in an impossibility.[6]

2. *"Stand firm."* Stand your ground. Don't give in to your fear and run away. Face your fear, allow yourself time to calm down, and then see the fear from God's perspective.

3. *"Be still."* Sometimes we are so frantic and noisy with our fear that we override God's direction, God's peace, and God's presence in our lives. We can be helped by quietly listening for His voice to guide us.

4. *"Move on."* This is what God said. When confronted with something we fear, we can run from it and give it control over us. Or we can face it, move toward it, and eventually neutralize it. When we fail to move on, we procrastinate, and procrastination is not God's plan for us. Procrastination is fear that has forgotten the promises of God. It is our effort to make life stand still for awhile when God has clearly instructed us to keep moving.

Another scriptural example is the story of the twelve spies Moses sent to spy out the Promised Land. (See Numbers 13.) The spies returned from their mission with two very different reports. Ten of the spies feared failure and voted to procrastinate because their enemies in the land were large and numerous. The ten complained, "We seemed like grasshoppers in our own eyes, and we looked the same to them" (Numbers 13:33).

The way you view yourself dictates the way you will act. If you see yourself as inadequate, you will be inadequate. Your fear becomes a self-fulfilling prophecy.

But Caleb and Joshua were ready to trust God and move on despite the odds. Caleb said, "We should go up and take possession of the land, for we can certainly do it" (Numbers 13:30). Going forward shrinks fears; procrastinating only enlarges them.[7]

☞Five Steps to Better Decision Making

How can you confront your fear of making decisions? What is the decision you're most fearful of making at this time? Apply the following questions to the decision you're struggling with at this time:

- What is the actual outcome I want from the decision?
- What are some alternative outcomes that may result from my decision?
- Where is my fear and lack of trust coming from?
- What can I learn from the decision-making process?
- This is what I will do to make the process more important than the outcome:

Remember: By not deciding, you are deciding to let something or someone else decide for you!

DECISIONS, DECISIONS, DECISIONS

At the beginning of the chapter, we discussed the fear of making a wrong decision, as illustrated by the paralyzed, wishy-washy game show contestants. If you were sitting in my counseling office and expressed your concern over making the wrong decision, I would probably respond by asking, "What's a wrong decision? What would make your decision wrong?" Interesting questions. I've asked them many times, and I've heard many responses. For example:

- "It was a bad decision because things didn't turn out the way I wanted."
- "The result of my decision wasn't what I was hoping for."
- "The decision is wrong when the results are upsetting or hurtful."
- "I'm not sure I can handle the results of a wrong decision."

All of these answers suggest that a decision is wrong based upon the kind of result it produces. Many fear wrong decisions because they fear the wrong results of their decisions.

But we place too much emphasis upon the *results* of our decisions and fail to realize the value of the *process*. Often what we call a wrong decision can be a right decision regardless of the results. I've made some decisions that produced results different from the ones I wanted. I've wasted time berating myself for my bad decision and wondering, *What would have happened if . . .*

Over the years, I've learned to ask myself questions that help me reinterpret my wrong decisions as decisions that enabled me to learn something I hadn't anticipated learning. Here are the questions I use:

- What was the actual outcome of the decision?
- Why was the outcome so bad? (Sometimes it can be classified as unpleasant and undesirable instead of bad.)
- What did I learn apart from the unexpected results?
- How am I a different person today because the results were different than I anticipated?
- What will I do differently the next time I face this decision?

It would be nice if every decision you made produced the results you wanted. But wrong decisions and their results are not the end of the world. Answering these questions can help you discover the good in a bad decision. This process may also help you realize that God has different plans in mind for you.

COURSE CORRECTIONS:
PART OF LIFE
Those who survive difficult situations and gain the most from life are those who are flexible and learn to adapt and change.

Stewart Emery, who wrote *Actualizations,* gives a helpful illustration of this process. During a flight to Hawaii, Emery rode on the plane's flight deck. One of the instruments that caught his attention was the inertial guidance system. The pilot explained that the function of the instrument was to guide the giant plane to within 1,000 yards of the runway within five minutes of the estimated arrival time. The system continually and automatically corrected the plane's course to achieve its programmed goal, even though the plane was off-course 90 percent of the time! The destination was reached by the process of making repeated course corrections.

We need to listen to and learn from our internal guidance systems and make the necessary course corrections in our lives. When we are not enjoying the desired outcome from our decisions, we either need to make a course change or learn to appreciate what we gain from the process of evaluating our decisions.[8]

MAKING THE MOST FROM YOUR MISTAKES

Most of us think of a failure as a negative experience. But we all fail at times, and we all make occasional mistakes. We can learn to use our failures to our advantage and to grow from them. Consider these guidelines for making the most from your mistakes:

1. *One mistake or failure does not mean everything is ruined.* Look for the success and achievement in every situation in which you experience a failure. If you cannot find the positives among the negatives, you're caught up in the fallacy of perfectionistic thinking. Whenever you feel you have failed, write down the areas in which you didn't fail. This exercise will help you keep the situation in proper balance.

2. *Mistakes provide us with excellent learning opportunities.* Most of us don't learn or grow unless we make mistakes. I've even heard some people refer to their mistakes as "corrective ventures" and "growth experiences." You can't outrun your mistakes, so turn around, face them, and learn from them.

3. *Failures help us adjust our behavior so we can get the results we want.* Failures can actually make things better. For example, in 1980 I took up racquetball. During the first four months, I made every mistake in the book and then some! I "failed" every game; I never won. But I kept working to improve my poor shots, and one day my failures paid off—I actually won a game. I still lose sometimes, but my failures help me focus on what I must do differently in the next game *not* to lose.

4. *Trial and error keeps you from getting paralyzed.* Have you ever sat with your legs crossed for a long period of time, then tried to stand and discovered that one leg was

asleep? For a few seconds, you were paralyzed, stuck, immobilized.

When you don't try anything for fear of failure, you are paralyzed. When you restrict your life so you don't make mistakes, you end up making the greatest mistake of all. You deny yourself the opportunity to develop all the capabilities God has given to you. He wants you to risk, to reach out. He would rather have you try and occasionally fail than to sit paralyzed by fear. And He is with you each step of the way.

5. *You can learn to live with imperfection.* I'd like you to write down on a separate sheet of paper a list of reasons that you're afraid of failure. I've heard many of them. Here are a few:

- "Other people will laugh at me."
- "Other people won't think much of me and will probably even get mad at me."
- "Other people won't like me."
- "If I make one mistake, I'll probably continue to make others."
- "God doesn't love me as much when I fail."
- "The feeling of failure is more than I can take. I just can't handle it."
- "When I fail, I confirm what my parents said about me. And I'm not going to do anything to prove them right!"

Every one of these reasons—including the ones on your list—can be challenged. You won't die or develop worms in your stomach when you make a mistake. Face it: You are imperfect, and you can learn to handle being imperfect.[9]

6. *The fear of failure will lift when you begin to view your life from God's perspective.* This is perhaps the most important suggestion of all. When you face a potential failure, ask God for His strength and wisdom to handle either the success or the attempt. Ask Him how you can use the failure for His glory and your growth.

Practical Steps for Overcoming Fear

Have you ever wondered why some people are able to overcome their fears while other people are overcome by their fears?

Terry and Hans, two men I counseled separately, illustrate this contrast. They were from nearly identical backgrounds, and they were both afraid of social activities and interaction.

But that's where their similarities ended. Terry gave in to his fear. Even though he desperately wanted friends and an active social life, he rarely mustered the courage to become involved. Hans, however, faced his fear and refused to be controlled by emotional thinking. As Hans stood up to his fears, they shrunk!

Hans overcame his fears by changing his thought patterns. "When I used to think about getting together with new people," Hans said, "I made all these put-downs about myself, like, 'I'll make a jerk out of myself' or 'No one will like me.' Now when those thoughts pop into my mind and start pumping up my fear, I counter them with realistic, positive thoughts. I think something like, 'I can be friendly and outgoing. People do feel comfortable with me. I can do it.'

"Another thing I often do," Hans continued, "is switch off my negative thoughts, tell myself to relax, take a deep breath, and tense up some muscles and then loosen them. I've found this really helps because my initial fear response tends to tense me up, even though I may not be fully aware of it. So I make myself become aware of the process and then consciously reverse it. I also spend time rehearsing in my mind how I see myself behaving and responding in a new social setting. I practice my social skills *in advance,* which helps build my confidence." Hans's simple method has worked for many.

GIVE YOURSELF TIME
TO OVERCOME FEAR
If you have lived with one or more particular fears for a long time, please remember it will take time to overcome. In fact, even after you have overcome a fear, you may still think you haven't. Does this sound strange? Perhaps, but when you have lived with a fear for so long, it is a major adjustment to begin living without that part of your life. Furthermore, a person who lives with a fear often learns to rely on other people in some way. So giving up that fear also means learning to be more independent.

Most fears need to be overcome gradually. Large or long-established fears are often too overwhelming to be conquered with one swift blow. Trying to conquer the fear immediately may actually cause the fear to grow instead of shrink. The best way to begin overcoming a fear is to face it a little at a time and from a safe distance.

Let's say, for example, that you have a fear of water. Throwing yourself headfirst into a swimming pool might help you overcome your fear. But for most people, the experience would be too traumatic. Wading into the water a little bit deeper each day will probably be more effective in the long run.

Sometimes I hunt pheasants with a large, black Labrador retriever—the kind of dog that often gets excited and jumps on people. Many little children (and some adults) are frightened by these large dogs. The steps for helping a child overcome his fear of a big dog illustrate the gradual approach each of us can use to overcome other fears.

Imagine a four-year-old boy meeting my black Lab for the first time. The huge dog runs up to the boy with his tail wagging and his tongue hanging out of a very large mouth between giant teeth. The dog is just being friendly, but the little boy is terrified by the sight of a dog that appears ready to devour him! The little boy flies to his mother, hides behind her, and cries. The next few times the dog approaches him, the boy has the same fearful reaction.

Then one day the boy retreats to his mother at the sight of the dog but doesn't cry. The next day, the dog is in the room, and the boy approaches the dog slowly and cautiously with his mother. The child eyes the dog and his big mouth warily from a distance. The boy's mother explains that the dog's mouth is open and his tongue is out because he is smiling and happy. Each day the pair moves two or three steps closer to the dog.

After several days, the boy gingerly puts his hand out and pats the dog's head. The dog's tail wags, and he stretches his neck out so the boy can scratch his head. In time, the boy examines the dog's mouth and teeth and realizes the big, black dog is not going to eat him.

How did the boy conquer his fear? By looking it straight in the mouth and gradually overcoming it! That's not always easy to do, but it brings results.

Sometimes a direct confrontation with fear *will* work to overcome it. I remember a personal story of fear told by Malcolm Boyd, author of *Are You Running with Me, Jesus?* When he was five years old, Malcolm's parents left him with a neighbor for the day. Malcolm did something to upset the neighbor, and her reaction was quite extreme. She struck him on the side of the head and locked him in a dark closet "where a huge white rat will eat you."

Young Boyd sat screaming in the darkness waiting for the rat to attack him. His sense of helplessness and terror at being in the dark persisted into adulthood.

As a middle-aged man, Boyd wanted to rid himself of this troublesome fear. He was asked by some friends to stay in their large and isolated home while they were away. After he moved in, Boyd decided this was the time to face his fear. As darkness fell one evening, he deliberately kept the lights off. When it was totally dark, he could hardly breathe from fear. But he began to feel his way slowly through the rooms of the house. He inched his way from the musty basement to the eerie attic. Gradually, Boyd became accustomed to and comfortable with the dark. His fears diminished, and today they are gone.[1]

Why don't people try the gradual approach to facing their fears? Because the idea just doesn't occur to them. They are too busy trying to avoid the object or situation that frightens them. And when they do decide to tackle the problem, they think they can lick it immediately, once and for all. The gradual approach to overcoming fear is foreign to many people. But it remains a highly effective method for conquering fears.

SETTING REALISTIC EXPECTATIONS

As you begin to conquer your fears, be realistic about your expectations. If you were to chart your improvement on a graph, it would not be a straight, upward line of uninterrupted success. Your growth will come in a series of ups and downs, and there will be times when your fears are actually worse.

You need to anticipate and plan for the down times. If you don't plan for your times of failure, you will be thrown by the apparent reversal in your progress. You will be tempted to think you haven't made any improvement at all, which isn't true. What you choose to focus on in those down moments will affect your whole attitude for the next two days.

If you are coming to grips with a long-standing fear that you have not confronted for many years, things could get worse at first. The fear can actually increase because you are coming closer to it. But overcoming your fear requires that you face and resist the sense of failure you will encounter in the process of getting involved with your fear.

STEP 1: IDENTIFY
YOUR PRESENT FEARS

If you want to succeed in overcoming your fear, you must develop a strategy for doing so. The first step of this strategy is to specifically identify what you fear.

You may respond, "That's easy; I'm afraid of people." But I'm not sure you are telling me exactly what you are afraid of.

Are you afraid of being rejected by people or attacked by people? Are you afraid of what people may think of you? What is it about people that makes you afraid?

Or you say, "I'm afraid to fly." But you still haven't told me exactly what your fear is. Are you afraid of being locked in an airplane's cabin or of being 30,000 feet off the ground or of crashing?

In each generally fearful situation, there can be a number of specific aspects to your fear, and these aspects must be identified. Once you have made specific identification, you can plan a specific strategy. This is part of the process Lloyd Ogilvie suggests when he says: "I confess my fearful imagination and today I ask the Lord to make my imagination a channel of His vision and not a breeding place of fear."[2]

Take a sheet of paper and write down a fear you have. For example, you may state your fear of elevators. Then list all of the different characteristics unique to your fear. You may write that you are afraid of being alone, being up high, falling, being locked in close quarters, meeting a stranger, or being alone with a person of the opposite sex. Some of your fears may have only one or two points, while others may have five or six.

Once you have listed your specific fears, rank them in order of importance, beginning with whatever you fear most.

STEP 2: DESCRIBE
YOUR FEAR HISTORY

Once you have identified and ranked your fears on a sheet of paper, write down the heading, "Past Experiences with This Fear." Then describe two or three times when you actually experienced this fear. Use the most recent experiences you can remember and give as many details as possible for these encounters. Then compare your description with the list of characteristics you previously identified for this fear to see if they coincide.

Can you remember what you actually said to yourself at the time you experienced your fear? Your statements may have included, "I feel awful," "I wish I was out of here," "This is a terrible experience," or "I can't handle this." Your self-talk under such conditions is very important because you could have inadvertently reinforced your fear response.

Be as specific as possible when listing your reactions to these past fearful situations. Did you become immobilized or did you run? Did you try to remain calm and confront your fear, or did you scream and run away? What did you feel when you last confronted your fear? Did your heart beat faster? Did you perspire? Did you feel like fainting or did your stomach begin to grind? List all the physical symptoms you experienced the last time you met your fear face to face.

☞Sample Worksheet

1. The object of my fear is . . .
2. The important characteristics of what I fear are (ranked in order of importance) . . .

   a.
   b.
   c.
   d.
   e.
   f.
   g.

3. My past experiences with this fear are . . .

   a.
   b.

4. My reactions to my fear were . . .

   a. What I said:
   b. What I did:
   c. What I felt:

5. How fearful was I? (Circle the number that best represents how you feel in the fearful situation: 1 means little or no fear; 5 means moderate fear; 10 means extreme fear.)

   1   2   3   4   5   6   7   8   9   10

STEP 3: BUILD A FEAR HIERARCHY

Regardless of what you fear, you need a plan to help you begin to overcome it. You have identified your fear in specific terms. Your next task is to plan a strategy for gradually approaching it and ultimately mastering it.

The strategy I recommend in this chapter is called building a fear hierarchy. It requires you to use your imagination in approaching the object, situation, or person you fear. You begin by imagining the least threatening situation in which you could involve yourself with this fear object. Gradually, you move to the most threatening scenario. Each imaginary scene in between builds upon those previous to it.

Here is a sample fear hierarchy that illustrates a gradual, scene-by-scene approach to overcoming fear. Notice how it begins with a low-threat scene and moves toward a direct confrontation with fear.

FEAR HIERARCHY FOR OVERCOMING THE FEAR OF FLYING IN AIRPLANES

1. I look at an advertisement for an airplane flight to Europe.
2. I look at color pictures of airplanes.
3. I visit an airport and look at the planes. While I am there, I see a friend or relative board a plane to go on vacation.
4. I call an airline to practice getting flight information.
5. I arrange with a local pilot to visit the airport and see a small private plane.

6. I visit the airport and see the planes. I sit inside the pilot's small plane while the engine is running. There is no attempt to fly the plane. I just get comfortable sitting in the cabin.
7. I imagine myself on a commercial jet plane getting ready for takeoff. The details for this and the remaining scenes I imagine are provided by a friend or relative who enjoys flying.
8. I imagine myself on a jet while it is in flight. I am with several friends or relatives.
9. I imagine myself on a jet while it is in flight. I am by myself.
10. I imagine myself on a jet while it is in flight. I am by myself, and the ride is somewhat bumpy.
11. I imagine myself on a jet by myself, and the plane is landing.
12. I take a short plane flight with a friend or relative.[3]

Remember that the fear hierarchy is a mental exercise; you are not facing the actual fear. The number of scenes or steps you have may vary depending on how many you need. The more gradual your approach to the fear, the more scenes you will want to include in your imagination.

It is vital to add one more procedure to each step in your fear hierarchy. Discuss your fear with God at each level and thank Him for giving you the peace you are going to experience. Ask Him to make your imagination a residence for His peace and presence.

The types of scenes you include in your hierarchy will depend on your circumstances and fears. For example, you can include in your imaginary scenes friends, relatives, or whoever you need to provide support and help in overcoming your fear. As you create a scene in your mind, begin with one that is only slightly unsettling to you. The fear must be small enough for you to be able to eliminate it in your mind and stay relaxed during this process. If your first scene creates too much fear and anxiety for you, back off and create one that is less stressful.

Below is an additional example. John was a college student who was petrified to speak in front of a class or a group at church. He wanted to be a schoolteacher, so he knew something had to be done to eliminate his fear. He committed himself to a program of creating visual imagery. Notice how John gradually builds up to a very fear-provoking situation for his final scene. Here is his list.

FEAR HIERARCHY FOR OVERCOMING THE FEAR OF SPEAKING TO GROUPS

1. I imagine myself reading from a book out loud with no one else in the room or likely to walk into the room while I am reading.
2. I imagine myself giving a practice lecture out loud at home when no one else is present and no one is likely to walk in.
3. I see myself recording my voice as I talk out loud. Then I listen to myself in the

safety of my room and list every positive point that I can about my presentation.

4. I see myself reading to my best friend out loud, and he keeps giving me compliments.

5. I practice reading out loud to three friends in my room for fifteen minutes.

6. I practice giving a brief lecture on the meaning of a passage of Scripture to one of my close friends in my room. Afterwards, he helps me with some suggestions, then I repeat the presentation, adding his suggestions.

7. I imagine myself giving this same presentation to several of my friends in my room. I see myself starting out a bit uptight, but then I relax and pretty soon there is no tension. The presentation goes quite well. Each friend tells me that I did a good job, and I feel good about the presentation.

8. I imagine myself filling in for one of the teachers at church in a high school class of five students. I see myself being not too nervous. After I meet each student, I give a brief devotional, and they listen to me. It goes quite well.

9. I attend a college conference with my friends. During an open meeting, I raise my hand and share my thoughts, which I have just rehearsed in my mind. Other people are interested and attentive to me, and then my friends all give me their responses.

10. I continue to speak up at meetings and set a goal of speaking at least three times in each meeting.

YOUR FEAR-REDUCING SCENARIO

Now it is time for you to begin this exercise. Copy the fear hierarchy outline on a separate sheet of paper, leaving plenty of space to write for each scene. List one personal fear you would like to eliminate from your life. Then briefly sketch in as many verbal scenes as you need to move you gradually from a safe scene to a solid confrontation with your fear. Don't be concerned if you have difficulty relaxing during the final scenes. This will come later as you mentally rehearse the whole process.

FEAR HIERARCHY FOR OVERCOMING THE FEAR OF_____*(your fear)*

Scene 1 (Remember: This scene should be very safe and simple with very little anxiety.):

Scene 2:

Scene 3:

Scene 4:

Scene 5:

Scene 6:

Scene 7:

Scene 8:

Scene 9:

Scene 10 (Continue with as many scenes as you need.):

The Final Scene (This scene should be one that could make you anxious or fearful if you actually performed it at this time.):

Now go back through what you have written and add specific details to make the imaginary experience even more realistic.

For example, imagine you have just arrived at Niagara Falls. Close your eyes and picture yourself at one of the viewing points. Imagine the scene as vividly as you can. Hold this image for fifteen seconds.

What was it like? Did you hear the roar of the water cascading down? Did you feel the breeze blowing and the mist on the air? What did the sky look like? Were there clouds, or was the sky clear? Were there other people around, or were you alone? How did you feel as you viewed this spectacular sight? Now perhaps you have an idea of what I mean by adding more details to your step-by-step scenario.

If the scenes you created are not based on a real event, it is important you see yourself as an active participant. And if they are real-life scenes, you must be an active participant in them as well. Be sure you don't just sit on the outside and observe as these scenes are passing through your mind. Put yourself into the scene as though you were actually there.

Here is an example of greater detail in John's revised plan for overcoming his fear of speaking in front of groups.

FEAR HIERARCHY FOR OVERCOMING THE FEAR OF SPEAKING TO GROUPS (REVISED)

1. I am alone in my room at the dorm. Standing in the middle of the room, I read out loud from three pages of a devotional book that I enjoy. I stand up straight, use proper breathing, and change my volume and tone of voice.

2. Now I use this same book as a resource, but this time I give a spontaneous talk as though I were speaking to other students or a class. I imagine that people are in my room, and I look from chair to chair as though each chair were filled. I try to feel what it would be like if there were real people there.

3. I now read or repeat to myself several passages of Scripture that remind me of the presence of God and the power of Jesus Christ in my life. I repeat Philippians 4:13, "I can do everything through him who gives me strength," and Jeremiah 33:3, "Call to me and I will answer you and tell you great and unsearchable things you do not know." I visualize Jesus Christ standing with me as I speak, and I continue to remind myself of His presence with me.

4. I repeat step 2, but this time I record my presentation and my friend listens to it. I make a list of what I can do to im-

prove it and give the devotional talk once again.

5. Now I am going to read out loud again. But this time my friend is there, and he is sitting about six feet in front of me. He is very relaxed, and an encouraging smile is on his face.

6. This time I am going to read again, but there are three of my friends sprawled about in my room. I am still somewhat comfortable. I relax, and before I begin I repeat the verses from step 3 concerning the presence and power of Christ.

7. Now I am back with my one friend, and this time I am giving a talk without notes. I talk for several minutes in a casual way, sharing what I remember from the book. Afterward, he gives me his positive suggestions, and I repeat the presentation.

8. I am at church, and I walk into a classroom where I am substituting for another teacher. I introduce myself to the students, and we chat for a bit. I see myself asking a very pertinent question to get their attention. I share my devotional with them. Not only are they interested, but they ask some insightful questions.

9. I repeat step 3.

10. I attend the college briefing conference at Forest Home Conference Center. I am in a group meeting of fifty students, and a discussion is in progress. I raise my hand to be recognized, then stand and share my thoughts on the topic at hand. People watch and listen, some nod in agreement, and there is general interest in what I say to them.

POSITIVE SELF-TALK

You have taken a tremendous step forward by creating your own fear hierarchy and filling it with details. This exercise will help you approach your fear in a very gradual manner. But there is one more step you must take that has to do with your self-talk or inner conversations. What you say to yourself at this time may make the difference between overcoming your fear and continuing to be overcome by it.

If your statements reflect negativism, you will not mature in your mastery over fear. For example, if John says, "I'm going to forget what I wanted to say and make a jerk of myself," or "I will never learn to talk in front of people," or "This is going to be too much for me," he will hinder his progress. But if he counters each negative statement with a positive alternative, he will relax. John could say, "This is a new situation, and I will learn how to handle it," or "I probably won't forget what I am going to say, and even if I do, I can just say I have frequent lapses of memory like most geniuses," or "I've learned all of my life, and it may take awhile, but I'll get there."

I have one more list for you—your self-talk list. On the next page list some of the typical negative statements you make whenever you find yourself in the situation you fear. Then, in the right column, list the statements you could make to help you cope with the situation and face your fear.

SELF-TALK

Past Negative Statements	Present and Future Positive Statements
1.	1.
2.	2.
3.	3.
4.	4.
5.	5.
6.	6.
7.	7.
8.	8.

True, this exercise is a bit complex and involves a lot of effort. But for many, this process has been very effective. It is a step toward overcoming your fear. And your fears *can* be overcome; that's a promise from God!

Notes

CHAPTER 1

1. Dr. Herbert Benson, *The Mind-Body Effect* (New York: Berkley Publishing, 1980).
2. Herbert Fensterheim and Jean Baer, *Stop Running Scared* (New York: Dell, 1978), adapted from pp. 41-42.
3. Susan Jeffers, *Feel the Fear and Do It Anyway* (Columbine, N. Y.: Fawcett Book Group, 1987), adapted from pp. 39-43.

CHAPTER 2

1. Dr. Connell Cowan and Dr. Melvyn Kinder, *Women Men Love—Women Men Leave* (New York: New American Library, 1987), adapted from p. 30.
2. Mike Mason, *The Mystery of Marriage* (Portland, Oreg.: Multnomah, 1985), p. 84.
3. Michael McGill, *The McGill Report on Male Intimacy* (San Francisco: Harper and Row, 1985), adapted from pp. 220-231.
4. McGill, *The McGill Report*, adapted from pp. 245-246.
5. Tim Timmons and Charlie Hedges, *Call It Love or Call It Quits* (Fort Worth, Tex.: Worthy Publishing, 1988), adapted from pp. 122-128.
6. David Viscott, *Risking* (New York: Pocket Books, 1979), adapted from pp. 64-68.
7. Viscott, *Risking*, adapted from pp. 75-79.

CHAPTER 3

1. David Viscott, *I Love You, Let's Work It Out* (New York: Simon and Schuster, 1987), adapted from pp. 123-127.
2. Lloyd John Ogilvie, *12 Steps to Living without Fear* (Waco, Tex.: Word, 1987), p. 133.

CHAPTER 4

1. Georgia Watkin-Lanoil, *The Female Stress Syndrome* (New York: Berkley, 1985), adapted from p. 73.
2. Lloyd John Ogilvie, *Lord of the Impossible* (Nashville: Abingdon, 1984), p. 90.
3. David Seamands, *Healing Grace* (Wheaton, Ill.: Victor Books, 1988), adapted from pp. 61-66.
4. Seamands, *Healing Grace*, p. 117.
5. Seamands, *Healing Grace*, pp. 115-116.
6. Ogilvie, *Lord of the Impossible*, p. 70.
7. Ogilvie, *Lord of the Impossible*, adapted from pp. 92-95.
8. Stewart Emery, *Actualizations* (Garden City, N. Y.: Dolphin Books, 1978).
9. David Burns, *Feeling Good* (New York: Signet Books, 1980), adapted from pp. 325-326.

CHAPTER 5

1. Malcolm Boyd, "How I Overcame Three Fears," *Parade*, 3 July 1988, adapted from p. 11.
2. Lloyd John Ogilvie, *12 Steps to Living without Fear* (Waco, Tex.: Word, 1987), p. 147.
3. Gerald Rosen, *Don't Be Afraid* (Englewood Cliffs, N. J.: Prentice-Hall, 1976), pp. 69-71.

About the Author

DR. H. NORMAN WRIGHT is founder and director of Family Counseling and Enrichment, a counseling center in Tustin, California. He is also founder and director of Christian Marriage Enrichment, a national training organization for lay leaders and pastors.* Norm is the author of more than fifty books, including *How to Talk to Your Mate, Understanding the Man in Your Life,* and *Always Daddy's Girl.* He and his wife, Joycelin, are the parents of two children.

* For more information on Family Counseling and Enrichment or Christian Marriage Enrichment, write 17821 17th St., Suite 290, Tustin, CA 92680.

hunt. Everything you need–from finding openings to closing interviews and accepting offers. 72-2858-0 $2.25

■ *Make Your Dream Come True* by Charles R. Swindoll. A look at the key ingredients necessary for launching your best ideas. 72-7007-2 $2.95

■ *Six Attitudes for Winners* by Norman Vincent Peale. Let an internationally known speaker and author help you replace fear, worry, apathy, and despair with courage, peace, hope, and enthusiasm. 72-5906-0 $2.95

■ *Surefire Ways to Beat Stress* by Don Osgood. A thought-provoking plan to help rid your life of unhealthy stress. Now you can tackle stress at its source–and win. 72-6693-8 $2.95

■ *When Your Friend Needs You* by Paul Welter. Do you know what to say when a friend comes to you for help? Here's how to express your care in an effective way. 72-7998-8 $2.25

Give a pocketful of wisdom to a friend. Give a Pocket Guide.

Action Plan for Great Dads	$2.25
Best Way to Plan Your Day, The	$2.95
Chart Your Way to Success	$2.25
Christianity: Hoax or History?	$2.95
Demons, Witches, and the Occult	$2.95
Facing Your Fears	$2.95
Family Budgets That Work	$2.95
Five Steps to a Perfect Wedding	$1.95
Four Secrets of Healthy Families	$2.25
Four Steps to an Intimate Marriage	$2.95
Getting Out of Debt	$2.95
Hi-Fidelity Marriage	$1.95
How to Really Love Your Job	$2.95
How to Talk to Your Mate	$2.95
Increase Your Personality Power	$1.95
Landing a Great Job	$2.25
Make Your Dream Come True	$2.95
Maximize Your Mid-Life	$1.95
Perfect Way to Lose Weight, The	$2.25
Preparing for Childbirth	$2.95
Raising Teenagers Right	$2.95
Sex, Guilt & Forgiveness	$2.95
Single Parent's Survival Guide	$1.95
Six Attitudes for Winners	$2.95
Skeptics Who Demanded a Verdict	$2.95
Strange Cults in America	$2.95
Surefire Ways to Beat Stress	$2.95
Temper Your Child's Tantrums	$2.95
Terrific Tips for Parents	$2.25
When Your Friend Needs You	$2.25
Working Mom's Survival Guide	$2.25
Your Kids and Rock	$2.95

Available at your local Christian bookstore or by mail.

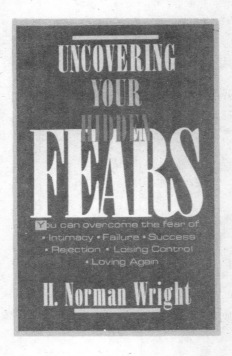